T0077375

# Still Smiling Through the Storm

## The heart of a girl who searched for love and comfort

By

S. LaTisha Branch

authorHOUSE®

AuthorHouse™
1663 Liberty Drive
Bloomington, IN 47403
www.authorhouse.com
Phone: 1 (800) 839-8640

Published by AuthorHouse  08/24/2015

ISBN: 978-1-4208-1597-9 (sc)

Library of Congress Control Number: 2004099218

Print information available on the last page.

Any people depicted in stock imagery provided by Thinkstock are models,
and such images are being used for illustrative purposes only.
Certain stock imagery © Thinkstock.

This book is printed on acid-free paper.

Because of the dynamic nature of the Internet, any web addresses or links contained in this book may have changed
since publication and may no longer be valid. The views expressed in this work are solely those of the author and do
not necessarily reflect the views of the publisher, and the publisher hereby disclaims any responsibility for them.

# Introduction

I HOPE YOU ENJOY THIS BOOK AS MUCH AS I ENJOYED WRITING IT. IT WAS MORE OR LESS A LIFE LESSON AND LONG JOURNEY AND I THANK EVERYONE WHO CHOSE TO TAKE THIS JOURNEY WITH ME. A LOT OF THESE POEMS WERE PERSONAL AND OTHERS WERE VERY CLOSE TO ME. I HAVE BEEN THROUGH A LOT OF HEARTACHE, MISTREATMENT, PAIN AND LOSS. I HAVE NEVER BEEN GOOD AT TALKING ABOUT BEING HURT OR WRONGED. SO, VERY EARLY IN LIFE I STARTED TO WRITE ABOUT THINGS, LIKE MY EXPERIENCES, MY WANTS, AND FEARS.

I EXPERIENCED A LOT VERY EARLY IN LIFE AND HAD NO CHOICE BUT TO HANDLE IT. I HAVE LOVED, LOST, LOVED AGAIN AND THOUGHT THAT I WOULD NEVER LOVE AGAIN. I LOST TWO CHILDREN AND GAINED THREE THAT I LOVE DEARLY. IT HAS NOT BEEN ALL BAD TIMES. WITH THE BAD CAME MORE GOOD. BUT I MADE IT THROUGH, IT WAS NOT EASY AND I WOULD NOT RECOMMEND IT, BUT MY FAITH GOT ME THROUGH IT AND SOMEHOW MADE ME A STRONGER PERSON.

I JUST HOPE YOU ALL UNDERSTAND THAT LIFE IS NOT PERFECT AND PEOPLE ARE NOT EITHER. SO BEFORE YOU JUDGE ME OR ANYONE ELSE THINKS TWICE ABOUT WHY PEOPLE ARE THE WAY THEY ARE, WHO MADE THEM THAT WAY AND WHAT THEY HAVE ACCOMPLISHED IN THEIR LIFE BECAUSE OF THESE THINGS. IF YOU DO NOT UNDERSTAND SOME THINGS IN THIS BOOK OR ABOUT ME, THAT IS OK, IF YOU DON'T AGREE WITH THIS BOOK OR ME THAT IS OK ALSO. JUST REMEMBER EVERYONE HAS AN OPINION AND EVERYONE IS ENTITLED TO IT, AND THIS IS MINE.

# Table of Contents

# My Father

As he walks through the door,

with his hat over his eyes

He strolls over to the sofa

with coat and hat still on.

Running his fingers over the remote control, he turns the channel.

He turns to "Father knows best"

Then he rises and goes to the kitchen

as he opens the refrigerator door,

he reaches for the beer in the back.

Coming from the kitchen

I still can't see his face.

As he walks to the door,

as walks back out of my life.

    S.L.Branch

    1/92

# Baby

Her soft round face
with the eyes opened wide
the little fingers on the hand
over the face to hide
the round belly just over
the belt so snug
the tiny little feet
on the soft rug.
On her hands and knees
she crawls so swift
on her back and side
she quietly drifts.

S.L. Branch
1/92

## Girl's Best Friend

Pressing my face on the windowpane,

Takes me down memory lane.

What do I see, yet two brown eyes looking back at me,

and I wonder just what it is they see.

A lonely little girl wanting a friend,

whose heart he knows he could win.

But no matter what they see,

in my arms is where he'll be.

So I picked him up, and paid the fare,

to take him home to give him tender loving care.

    S.L.Branch

    1/92

## You don't have to be alone

Sitting on our sofa at home,

having no company just being all alone.

Working all day, with no fun or no play,

is not helping you along life's narrow way.

Open your heart to a friend not a foe,

then your life will be on the go.

    S.L.Branch

    1/92

# Your friendship alone

I'm not asking for anything from you
just your friendship will do.
Someone to listen when you just need to talk,
or someone to go to when you just want to walk.
Someone you can pick up the phone and call,
so you don't have to build that great big wall.

> S.L.Branch
> 1/92

# Lonely Stone

One little stone on the sand
One little stone in my hand
hold it in the sunshine's beam
watch it glow, shimmer and gleam.
Sitting alone on the shore,
waiting to get to the ocean floor.
So holding on to this lonely stone,
listening to the seas low moan.
Throwing this stone into the moaning sea,
and watching it sink to the ocean floor, just like me.
> S.L.Branch
> 12/94

# Come Home to me

The days seem longer and longer
as I wait to see your face

It seems like forever
until I feel your warm embrace.

I long to have you close to me
and never let you go.

Time never seems to past
too fast just slow.

Your journey may be
by land or sea.

It does not matter
as long as you "Come home to me"
S.L.Branch
10/95

# Friends for now

Feelings are still being mixed
like a freshly made stew
thoughts are still settling
like newly formed dew
words are being chosen
with the utmost care
friends will stay friends
as long as they dare.

    S.L.Branch
    9/95

# Been There and Back

I've cried an ocean of tears
I've lied awake sleepless nights.
I've watched the phone never ring.
I've sat at home alone, and listened to the wind moan.

But things will never get better.

I will cry no more
I will sleep a peaceful sleep
I will call you back instead.
I will go out on the town and try never to frown.

S.L.Branch

8/95

# Love Addiction

Symptoms of withdrawal
come from not being able
to touch you, hear you.
Feeling you inside me as
the first time we made love.
The enjoyable pain...
The hurt you can bare...
Feelings like you can't live another day.
This amazing thing called love,
the quick fix...

                    S.L.Branch
                    6/95

# Vibes

I see your face
when I sleep at night
I hear your voice
ring in my ear
I smell your cologne
in my clothes when I undress
I feel your presence
which makes me feel safe
when I drift into
a coma like place.
S.L.Branch
6/95

# A Visit To Ecstasy

I live many fantasies
no matter what the realities
I see us in bed
not one word being said.
As our lips meet
our hearts rapidly beat.
Our bodies combined as one
my mind and soul you've won
after it was said and done
regrets were thought by no one.
S.L.Branch
5/95

# Table for 1

The bowl I see
filled to the rim

The plate to me
is nice and trim.

The tall blue cups
with drinks to fill

The napkin; like sleeping pups
sit so still.

     S.L.Branch
     5/95

# The Pain I Feel

The pain I feel
is like a dagger
lodged in my heart so deep

The pain I feel
is like a river
run dry from drought

The pain I feel
is like a baby
who has no one to love him.

The pain I feel
is like no other pain I've felt,
which is why this pain hurts so bad.
S.L.Branch
5/95

# A Man's Desire

If a son is what you desire,

then I shall light your fire.

Your love is all I long for,

wanting to feel you more and more.

Your body is asking for attention,

and I want to give you all of my affection.

S.L.Branch

2/95

# Never Find Another

The hurt I feel when I see you with another

should make me go find another brother

but the love I feel will never pass

I should hope this love would never last

I don't know what steps to take,

to make you see all the rest are fakes

my feelings for you are deeper than you know

therefore what you do to me is low

the things I do for you

are things they will never do.

S.L.Branch

1/96

# My Rose Garden And I

As the mist falls

on the petals of a rose.

The leaves of a stem

weighed down by the water

as it is pulled by the stem

from the dirt.

The roots wave

to the newly exposed sun.

as it peeks from behind the clouds

the sun smiles brightly

over the rose garden and I.

S.L. Branch

1/96

# Thoughts Of Innocent Friends

As you lay me on the bed so made,

my body I want you to raid.

From the back or from the front,

the pain I feel is not sharp yet blunt.

This is a good and easy pain,

the kind that keeps you sane.

I want this pain both night and day,

when it comes bring it all the way.

S.L.Branch

1/96

# I Am

When I look in the mirror I see,
a strong, ambitious woman looking at me.
Tall yet full in every way,
with a big bright smile to make your day.
The deepness of her dimples,
and the appearance of not one pimple.
From the profound line of her lips,
to the curve of her hips.
Down the length of her leg,
like a bone would make any dog beg.
This personality and body can satisfy any man,
like any strong woman can.

S.L.Branch

5/97

# Dear Lord

Praying again to my father in heaven,
that things will get better for me
as I fall to my knees with arms open wide,
I ask "Dear Lord" from this let me hide.
You watch over me both night and day,
but in my defense, I'd hope you 'd say...
Release this child from the hole she's in,
and place her where she can begin again.
And this "Dear Lord" I ask today,
that you will just make a way.

S.L.Branch

'98

# Fascination

Why am I so fascinated by what's behind that door?

Why do I stare and glare through that window more and more?

I see his face when I close my eyes,

and hear his voice when it's not wise.

This man, you see, that fills my head,

has already dawned someone else's bed.

But his smile, his walk and his every touch,

makes me feel that this is too much

I want to close my eyes and him disappear,

so when my feelings coming out I won't fear.

Now I know why I'm fascinated with what's behind that door,

because there is someone behind that door that I did adore.

S.L.Branch

'98

# The Baby (Sable)

When you came into our lives,
you were so young and shy.
Just taken from your mother we never heard you cry
with a body so small and black,
my ultimate goal was to send you back
as you started to grow and wanted to be held,
our bond of closeness began to weld.
The more I disliked you for the way you came,
the more I grew to love you and you loved me the same.
As the time goes by your smile I can't resist,
you are the #1 dog on my list.

S.L.Branch

'98

# Must Say Goodbye

Please don't think less of me because I don't cry,
even though I'll be missing you, I don't want to say goodbye.
They say that space is a virtue, and time is of the essence,
yet all I want is to be in your presence.
S.L.Branch

'98

# Dinner's Served

Hold me

Touch me

Lay me down

Mount my body

Enter my gates

Gently thrust

Moan and groan

Rivers flow

Climax reached

Kisses down

In and out

Suck and lick

Appetizer, open wide

Eat up

Dinner's served

S.L.Branch

9/98

# Intercourse

As my pleasure gate opens wide,
I wait for you to come inside.
With your gentle thrust,
this feels more than lust
Feeling your body next to mine,
with juices flowing like fine wine.

S.L. Branch

6/98

# Could It Be?

There's a guy I met to my surprise,

As he began to talk the hair on my neck started to rise

The sight of him made my flesh crawl and my brow sweat,

But my guard down and emotion show, I can't let.

Be a friend and a listening ear,

this is what I am when he is near.

But when he is away,

He is on my mind at night and all day.

A significant other he has and says he loves,

but when we are together we fit like hands in a glove.

He brings the life out of me, I never knew I had,

Yet feeling the way I do sometimes I feel bad.

More than a friendship may never be,

but he will always have a friend in me.

    S.L.Branch

    7/98

# The Man I Knew

As the years go by, with ups and many more downs,

the man of my dreams finally made me frown.

The fate that brought us back to stay,

we watched that fate slowly fade away.

I felt he was the world, with no wrong in sight.

Yet all of a sudden he brought the darkness in night.

The memories I store on that shelf in the back,

those are the memories; it's just to hard to pack.

Feeling as though my heart was beating out of my chest,

my feelings for you just won't let me rest.

As the words crossed my lips, and the crack broke my heart,

I turned and made a step to a brand new start.

I said I hate you and I want you to go,

But when you do leave and don't try to stay, you hurt me so.

S.L.Branch

7/98

# No Visitor For Me

As I sit at my window and watch the day pass,

I often wonder exactly what's on the other side of the glass.

I see cars come and I see them go,

but through all the traffic I don't see you though.

As time is told by the sun going down,

not seeing you ride in my court only makes me frown.

As I close that shade with no visitor for me,

I wonder will there ever again be, a we.

S.L.Branch

6/98

# The Man I Knew cont.

More that a decade ago,
I met a man that never did let go.
We went through ups and even downs,
now his goal is to never see me frown.
Finding each other was nothing more than fate,
I now felt it was well worth the wait.
Simple bliss I feel I've found,
now in my life I'm homeward bound.
Although when reality sets in again,
the memories of you I have in my brain.
Stored away in a safe and secure place,
So that when all is calm I can open and embrace.
The smile that comes at the mention of his name,
Is a sure sign that this is no game.

S.L.Branch

5/98

# Aunties Boys

One in the arms and one on his own,

two little bundles with mother alone.

No father in sight but family all around.

Two little angels so innocent you see,

will grow up to be liberal and free.

With no father in sight but family all around.

Intelligence and honors in their future to be,

these little boys will make me a very proud auntie.

With no fathers in sight but family all around.

S.L.Branch

5/98

Demetrius (D.J) & Deondre' (Dre') on Sunday Morning in white shirts and blue pants, Dre is taller.

D.J.'s school picture in a blue/white shirt with bugle boy on the front.

Dre's school picture in a light blue shirt with bugle boy on front.

# You Are

You are the man in my life

You are the stride in my step

You are the twist in my walk

You are the pitch in my voice

You are the twinkle in my eye

You are in the height of my head

You are the light in my life

S.L.Branch

5/98

# What I Want

As I look into your deep brown eyes,

Visions of you I see by my side.

Know this is something I want to be,

not knowing if this is something that can be done.

I want you beside me in good and bad.

I want to make you mine forever more.

You are my shelter from harm.

S.L.Branch

1/98

# Don't Go

As I lay on the pillow,

tears stained the case.

With a heart that's torn like a delicate piece of lace

The pain shoots through like a dagger through a stone.

Feeling as though you've left me all alone.

The emptiness I feel when I don't here your voice,

makes me feel I never again will rejoice

               S.L.Branch

               11/99

# Feel Me

When you touch the small of my back
I want you closer than ever before
When you move up to my neck and below
My temperature starts to rise and soar
As you glide down the arch of my legs
I want you deeper and deeper
Tracing my body from head to toe
Makes me feel there is a fire burning
Hotter than anyfire ever made.
That just can't be put out

S.L.Branch
5/98

# Want That Back

Mentally pushing rewind on my mind
I go back to where I want to be
that place I was just the other night
when I was calm, quiet and free
hovering above my body as if I were the last angel
I could see just what was meant for me
the pleasure I felt, the bliss of passion
where did I go? I will never know
wherever that place is just holding my slot
one day I'll be back to enjoy bliss again
S.L.Branch
11/99

# Missing You

When I look at my computer screen
I see your face, so clear and near
When we are apart I want to be near you
just to get a glimpse of your smile
Your dimples, and your deep brown eyes
I hear your voice in my head
smell your scent on my body
Feel when your not there
What am I to do about this want
Just one minute is all it takes
for that urge to be satisfied
just one glance, just one kiss
that would linger on forever

S.L.Branch
11/99

# Is This For Me

When I look in your eyes I know what I want
putting it in words is the hardest thing to do,
When all I want is to be near or around you.
I don't know what my feelings are saying
When my stomach does somersaults and twirls,
My heart races and I sweat and loose all my curls.
I feel like I have never felt before
feeling like this is what god has in store for me,
I just hope I am seeing what he wants me to see.
I have given and given so much that I am scared
Scared to receive, when disappointment is always there,
You always think life is just unfair.
Holding on to that heart so tight,
not letting anyone in with out a fight.

S.L.Branch

11/99

# You Belong To Her

When you'll call her back later,

or when you just have to make a run.

You belong to her...

When you don't call right back,

or just go into the other room.

You belong to her...

I know were I stand when you say,

"I'm just talking to one of the guys".

You belong to her...

When you are questioned and answer,

each and every question.

You belong to her...

When the people walk and look,

and we move or stop conversation.

You belong to her...

When you can't be away from home,

and not answer a page or call without catching grief.

You belong to her...

When your car can't be at another house,

or another car can't be at your house.

You belong to her...

How do I know? Because what she wants she gets,

as the great Malcolm X said, "By any means necessary".

And until you stop the vicious circle, you will belong to her.

S.L.Branch

½5/00

# My Story

Once upon a time there was a girl, who was a special girl,

She would give people anything they needed if she could.

She loved people, all kinds of people, she also loved love,

this girl was a dreamer; she wanted the world and everything in it.

She worked from the time she could start to now,

She also worked on her life with men.

She started with younger men then older men, no one could handle her,

and She gave and gave of herself, until they eventually left her.

Blaming herself each and every time, she promised to do better,

during the next relationship she worked on making the man happy.

All the while she neglected herself, she gave when needed,

and never asked for anything for herself.

She always believed that a woman makes her man happy.

Years went by and men also came and went,

this girl became a woman, and fell from likes to loves.

She got into her first real relationship, so she thought,

with a guy she sought after since grade school.

She did everything she thought in her power to make him desire her, and

appreciate what she did,

but that 5 year, span of her life seemed hopeless.

Then one day her rainy skies seemed to go permanently sunny, when she

met a man, a man who she could talk to, that made her laugh and smile.

The only downfall was this man worked with her and was legally separated

with two children,

and he had a life that she would take second too for a while.

This woman kept her guard up but she went out with him and had the time

of her life,

This man really seemed to care and he never made her feel like second even

though he had others in his life.

There was always time for her, she felt a love that no one had ever given her,

this man brick by brick took that wall down and she handed him her heart.

She asked questions and made pleas for him to take her heart with ease,

for this is her last hope of finding that man to make her happy.

Her life seemed to be at an all time high, so high she felt something was wrong,

She told him she was concerned he assured her he would never hurt her and

it was over.

That is really all she wanted to hear, she gave herself to him, and spoke

those three important words "I Love You".

From then on she was completely devoted to him, and what he wanted,

when there was something wrong she listened and gave encouragement and support.

They did things together that she had never done and that made her feel

like a woman,

it was like he knew exactly what she needed and wanted.

They would come home and maybe eat maybe not,

just sit and talk when that was what one of them needed to do.

That was what she wanted to be a partner to a great man,

and have him love her and respect her, and not be afraid to be seen with her.

The time together started to get farther and farther apart, and she felt in

her heart that something was wrong.

All the dancing at night, sitting and talking, and laying in each other's

arms, going out with each other,

and leaving little notes of affection and admiration dwindled, stopped

or just ceased.

The dreams, and happiness that this woman enjoyed with this man,

is taken away at the blink of an eye, and at a split second.

She feels as though her heart has stopped, and she can't breathe,

and why would she want to, the man she loved and gave her heart to

for the very last time is gone.

Wondering if there is anything she could do to get the love of her life back,

but knowing that he may never love her that way again.

Her life and dreams are over.

S.L.Branch

2/12/00

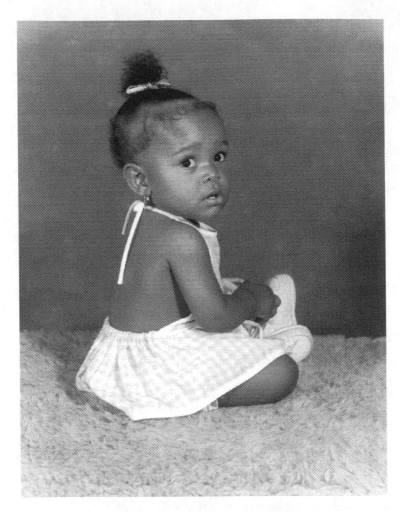

Picture of me at 10 months in a pink-checkered dress with the back out.

My grandfather holding me in at the alter in our church, Emanuel A. M. E Church.

A school picture of me in high school, I. C. Norcom High School.

My debutante picture for The Progressive Women Inc. in a gown

Me at 20 years old.

Me and Kevin my confidant.

# Deep Hurt

Throw daggers

penetrate my heart

squeeze the wound

catch the blood

buckets at a time

take it to the water

dump it in and watch

watch it disappear

as so will I

Like water missing from a well

day by day

little by little

I too will be gone

watch me as I fade away

S.L.Branch

   8/15/00

# (Not) Meant To Be

Years ago, I opened my heart for you to come in,
you stood and stared and waited to compare.
I sat and waited and did what I could,
I was your wife without that piece of paper,
yet, none of this did me any good.
You had it all and did not see it there.
Then one day someone else came and took me,
and at that moment your eyes opened to see.
My absence made you feel like hell
You changed and did it all to get me back,
but after my return your new lease on love became slack.

S.L.Branch

4/00

# What More Do You Want

I try to be there being by your side

console and listen and eyes open wide.

In your corner fighting with you

all this and stay invisible too.

Staying out of sight so no one knows

the woman, who to battle for you goes.

For your cause she is a rebel for you,

staying honest and true.

What more could you ask for in a friend,

who is willing to go beyond and more than a hand lend.

Call anytime day or night to talk, or just sit,

she will never give you grief or a fit.

What more can she do,

to prove devotion to you?

    S.L.Branch

    2/17/00

# How Would You Know

How would you know
if I left this lonely place
stopped running this tiresome race.
After you've played house and done what you do,
you pause for a minute to check on me too.
But this time I'm not there,
and no one knows or even seems to care.
So I did what I do best, when I am left alone for so long,
I leave and go to a world were nothing could go wrong.
A place where I will be loved by all, and hurt by none,
and will be appreciated for the long race I've won.
I won't have to be seen for people to care ,
and around for them to be aware.
If I leave this place then I won't have to feel pain,
the down side is I also won't have to love again.
So you don't have to worry about me,
because with my father I will be.

S.L.Branch
2/17/00

# No Man 4 Me

He walked out of my life before I was here
to say I forgive you or that I even care.

He left and never turned back to see my face,
to see what he contributed to this earthly place.

He never called and never asked what is it, boy or girl,
that I have in this world.

He walked into my life as a figure for me to see,
not to feed, clothe, and house me.

He did what was expected and wanted at the time,
he came and did whatever at the drop of a dime.

I thought this man was the one that would stand by me,
and support me in every way and make our family a we.

Then the number one man in my life,
that gave me love, happiness and never strife.

He gave his love unconditionally to me,
and everyone else had a price you see.

I was his heart, his soul, his doll in a glass case,
that no one can hurt, and no one can replace.

He protected me all he could, then opened the door and let me go,
so I could find that one man that could make me happy and not feel low.

That man appeared and made me smile, and feel like the world was mine,
he gave me things that money could not buy and I felt as though I would
always be fine.

He gave me his time, his support, his heart, his shoulder and his love,
we sat and talked for hours and bonded so well we fit like hand in glove.

My heart I gave this man, more than I gave any man,
he took it and held it until from me he was band.

His heart seemed to be hurting, but I was neglected in the mean time,
wanting to be with him and make this man happy and mine.

Watching him hurt and be manipulated how can I make it better, make
it stop,
make it better for us and help the fear and pain to drop.

Lord help obtain the life I want with the man I love, and let him see
the love he has in me,
my lovers name is poppie he is the love of my life and the only man I see.
S.L. Branch

# Thank Me

Thank me, for giving you the time of day,

Thank me, for trying to show you the way.

Thank me, for giving you the time of your life,

Thank me, not being just like your wife.

Thank me, for covering your ass in time of trouble,

Thank me, for being there for you on the double.

Thank me, for doing what most people would not do,

Thank me, for trying to love you,

Thanking me, for this time is what you should do.

S.L.Branch

2/18/00

# Out of Control

You walk around with your ass in a roar

but your true obsession is with the vision you have

you know more than you want to know

just what your anger is letting you show.

You want him no more or no less

but to let him go would be not your best.

Knowing someone showed you up

you know nothing more than you must interrupt.

I don't want him, but you can't have him is what

    you must prove

by doing all you can to try and stop this groove.

This battle you may have won

but your personal war has just begun.

I don't have to wish it upon you

because you will get what is due.

                S.L.Branch

                2/18/00

# Why???

How could you do it, how could you say,

the things and words to me this day

I gave you nothing but love, and protected you

all the way.

Covered your name, character and pride,

with theses things in mind, I uncovered my hide,

but none the less, no more harm for you just

the tears I cried.

Putting me on the line, I hope it saved you,

and made her feel better about controlling you too,

the only control she has is of what you say and do.

Hurting you both I have no intention of,

because the pain you will receive will come from above;

for I know I did nothing wrong but give a man who

needed it my love.

S.L.Branch
2/18/00

This part of my book is basically started after the death of my Aunt, Vanessa Faye Ruff, and my grandfather, Herbert Lee White. I kind of started to feel like I was so alone and my protection and support was gone. I am a very independent woman as of lately. When I was growing up, my family, especially the men did almost everything for me. The drove me places, they bought things, and other things that needed to be done. I was spoiled I guess. But after these deaths, I started to grow really fast. I started dating a very productive and special man. He was older and as so many before him he took care of me.

Before my aunt and grandfather died, I had my first miscarriage. That was the day that I met this man. We knew of each other, but when he discovered the father did not want an parts of this baby, he decided to stay with me. He has been with me every since that day. So the emotion is from all the lost I was experiencing through this time. Then three years later God saw fit to call my father and then my grandmother home.

For the last four years I have thought from time to time that I can't live feeling like this. It hurts too much, then I look at my mother who is a survivor and I look at those three babies that I am raising and I have to believe that he is keeping me here for a reason. I don't know what it is and maybe it is not time for me to know. I have to believe that my faith, my prayers, my family and the knowledge that my grandma and grandpa, my aunt and my daddy are in heaven taking care of my babies. My aunt left behind a husband as well as a daughter, Calvina. She has been my right hand, more like another sister, my best friend. She also never stopped, we have days and we both understand each other.

So when you think that there is nothing left to live for, think again about your family, the children and that person who loves you unconditionally. Talk to someone, write it out, draw it out, and just get it out.

# Calling Home An Angel

On that day our lord and savior said,

Vanessa my child I've made your bed.

She replied "Dear Lord", please not yet,

my family's needs are not quite met.

They need me to help; they need me to guide,

sometimes they just need me to confide.

I'm the knee baby of three,

and they often rely on me.

I'm the aunt to two,

who always has things for me to do.

I'm the mother to a little girl,

who needs me in her world.

Not to mention the wife of a man,

who relies on my helping hand.

Vanessa, now that I know what you want me to do,

I will make your wish come true.

In my name I promise you,

in time, your family will make it through.

Now come my child it's time to rest,

for your family, you've done your best.

With no more pain, but eternal peace,

their love for you will never cease.

Dear lord, one last thing before I go,

I am not leaving Calvina, please let her know.

Along with my family, I'll be with her everyday,

and still guide and help her along the way.

With all this, it's time to lay my head,

in the place you made, my heavenly bed.

S.L.Branch

8/12/00

Aunt Nessa at 23 years old.

Aunt Nessa with Calvina before she passed.

Uncle Calvin and Calvina at college graduation on Mother's day. I know Aunt Nessa was so proud

# God Don't Make No Mistakes

When the sun shines and there is no rain in sight,
or when the clouds come and it looks like night.
God Don't Make No Mistakes.
When a child grows up and wants to move away,
or gets mad at you and has nothing to say.
God Don't make No Mistakes.
When he removes our loved ones from our life,
he answers our prayers and removes all from strife.
God Don't make No Mistake.
When I cried "Dear Lord, why did you take him away."
My momma said, "he'll still be with you everyday".
Because God don't make no mistakes.
I'm here today to let you know,
we hurt because he had to go.
But God don't make no mistakes.
So when you shed a tear for me,
just remember that I now see.
That God don't make no mistakes.

S.L.Branch

8/18/00

Grandma in her floral dress.

Granddaddy & Grandma on their 50th anniversary.

Aunt Althea,Consuelo(mom) and aunt Vanessa on top from left to right, then Timithea, Calvina and myself.

Aunt Althea, me, Consuelo(mom),uncle Calvin, Deondre (below me), Timithea, Calvina, Alma(grandma), and Demetrius. (Daisha is born a month after this picture, Timithea is 8 months here).

# A Christmas Gift

When I smile and laugh I fill my heart with love

When you kiss me hello or kiss me goodbye

you help maintain that full heart

your touch, your smile, and loving words

all maintain this heart of mine

all the money in this world

could not give me what you have

there is nothing that I could buy

to show you my love

so to you I give the only thing

that only I can give you

that no one else can give you

"My Heart"

It has been broken a few times

and it has been walked on

but I brushed it off and put it back in

then it was torn apart and battered and worn

but still I mend it, patched it

and put it back once more

it makes me who I am and helps me to love

so after shopping and searching the malls and catalogs

I decided what your biggest Christmas gift would be

I give you "My Heart"

so now you have all of me

my love, my body and soul

and now it is official because you have

"My Heart"

       S.L.Branch

       12/22/01

# Wanted

You are there for me in my time of need

and you make everything go away

you somehow make it better

without having anything to say

I rely on you to get me through

my days and nights with ease and no pain

as I hold you in my hand

I know that in a short while

I will feel nothing

no hurt no pain no disappointment

you are the only one that never fails me

always by my side with the results I crave

you work part-time, no benefits, no raises

you work when needed, no set schedule

but you are a hard worker and you get the job done

and right now you hold this part-time position

but I look forward to the day

that I can hold you and say

"You are fired" and "I want you out of my life for good"

S.L.Branch

12/22/01

# Hurting Heart

As the days pass I long to see you
I just want one more day, one more night
I want to look into your brown eyes
I ache to have you hold me in your arms
or just to hear you whisper that you love me
my heart races in anticipation of a glance, a sound
the longer it takes
I feel like my heart stops beating
like it hurts to much to beat without you
then I see you and my heart gets a jump
which makes it able to beat just a little while longer
S.L.Branch
12/22/01

# My Time With You

It seems as though the days and nights get longer

our time together gets shorter

my feelings for you get deeper

my heart expands and gets wider


Then I ask why? Why do I love and loose?


The time we spent together was the best there ever was.

The time we spend together now just seems that it goes by so fast.

I love just being with you, spending time with you

I am at the point that if you just have to go out

to run errands, then I would go just to be with you

I realize that this is not good, but you showed a

genuine interest in me that most of my suitors never showed.

I survive off of attention and when I don't get it I am not happy.

That is why I am scared with everything that is about to change with us

I try to keep myself from a lot of heartache if possible

lately I have not done that

you cope a little better than me, due to the fact that

you have other obstacles to occupy yourself, but

I still love you and that is going to be the hardest thing

that I have to consider in all this

no matter what I just want you to remember that

I WILL LOVE YOU NO MATTER WHAT.

S.L.Branch

12/01

# 9/11/01

On that day someone took two obstacles

and put them in our way

using them as weapons to crumble

important figures for people this day

the figures first shook, then got weak

they swayed and buckled and fell to the ground

that day we lost a good portion of our nation

we did not loose our faith, or humanity

or our compassion, or our unity

they tried to take more than the figures

they aimed for

they aimed for our hearts, and missed

they aimed for our souls, and missed

they hit some structures and took some lives

but they can not take our pride

when things like this happen

you just want things the way they once were

on the day before when no one would have ever imagined

that someone would be so cruel

so mean, so heartless

so non-human

maybe they are not human

something inhuman that could

take lives and never look unsettled

they do make you wonder, wonder and pray

pray to God just to see another day

S.L.Branch

10/30/01

# Blacker Than Me

You braid your hair and add some beads,
or just loc it up and use oils
Does that make you blacker than me

You say you don't eat pork,
but season your meat in ham hocks or bacon grease
does that make you blacker than me

You smoke weed and say it is natural and from the earth
and light incense
does that make you blacker than me

You read some books and say you're from the "motherland"
But born in P-town (Portsmouth that is)
Does that make you blacker than me

So what makes you blacker than me
not your hair

What makes you blacker than me
not the food we eat

what makes you blacker than me
not what we inhale - or not

What makes you blacker than me
not what we think or say

We are from no "Mother Land",
but the queen our mother
that is what makes us the same
black is black.

S.L.Branch

10/30/01

# Sanctuary

It's a special place where tears form and fall
where your soul can hurt and no one knows
where you go when a storm comes
and you can get away
leaving this hell on earth
to be with my father
the only man that can save me
and
never desert me

S.L.Branch
10/02/01

# Pain Beyond

Tears falling, pain in my head
pain feel unbearable better off dead
chest feels swollen, hurting and tight
so tired of crying I can't even fight
wanting her to feel the pain that I do
wanting her to suffer and hurt too

S.L.Branch
10/2001

# Life Without

A day with no sunshine is my day without you,

flowers with no rain is how I feel when your not here.

A child with no parent is how it feels when I'm not in your arms,

like a puppy on a short leash, when I can't reach out and touch you.

Everything needs something else just to get by,

you are my reason, and you are my natural high.

S.L.Branch

11/2001

# Best Wishes

On the day your daughter was born,

you and your husband I must warn,

God sent you one of his angels full of love,

so enjoy your gift from above.

I am sending this gift for;

"Little Miss Daisha"

Who I know is full of fun.

I wish your family all the best.

And you guys will receive the rest.

S.L.Branch

11/2001

# Our Little Star

From the day you were born
between you and your brother we were torn
you are the youngest of two,
but there is nothing you won't do.
You are full of life and full of love,
and you are God's gift from above.
You are our prince to turn into a king,
and from our mouths your name will ring.

S.L.Branch
6/2001

Daisha in her red suit with black trim with the hat to match.

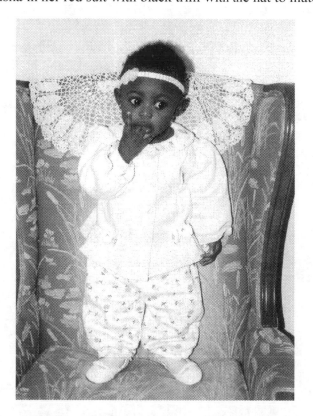

Daisha in her pink outfit standing in a chair.

Daisha (my princess) in a pink shirt that says "Cheer 84" at 2 years old.

Through all the deaths and sickness my family has endured over the last 5 years. The toughest part for me was when my mom was going through Breast Cancer. I think the chemo and the radiation made me as sick as it made her. I took her to the appointments, stayed in the hospital with her and watched her loose weight, hair and energy. I thought my mom was fading. At this time my family was dwindling and I had to keep it together. I would smile and try to keep her upbeat and cry when I was alone. Being as positive I could be I still could not loose my rock. But through all that sickness and pain, my mom never stopped smiling. So she was a big part of what got me through helping her. If she could smile then so can I. Today, my mom and I are the matriarchs of the family now. I always say that god knew what he was doing when he left her here. He looked down and said "Jan, Tisha is not quite ready for you to go."

The pictures after this poem, you will see are of my mother when she was going through treatment and all her hair came out.

# It's Me Lord

As I lay me down to sleep

I pray dear lord ours souls do keep

to keep us safe from hurt or harm

and to keep us both happy and warm

by the way dear lord I would like to know

Just how long am I going to have to keep letting go

I cherish the time I have and replay memories in my head


But I just can't help to want you with me instead

To care for you and to see you smile

That alone gets me through any trial

If I could put any problem you have in my hand

I would turn it into sand

Then blow it all away

So that we could be together from this day

But if we are called before we wake

I ask thee lord our souls to take

to heaven for us to rest

together in our heavenly nest.

S.LBranch

3/23/02

Mommy at an early age.

Mommy going through Breast Cancer when she lost her hair (and still smilin').

Me and my mommy (the cancer survivor) in white shirts.

Mommy and Daddy after the joy of two girls.

Mommy and Daddy with Dre' at a school function.

# Don't Leave

When you leave me

all I want is one more minute

just one more to hold you

just one more to kiss you

goodbyes can be good

but only when they are understood

assurance is the key

just how long will it be

will I see you tomorrow, or next week

will I get to lay with you, or just get a peek

the time apart seems like a lot

I feel like I'm not all there when you are away

I don't expect you to be in my presence everyday

you are my best friend

my support

my rock

and for you I try to be the same

sometimes I feel like

you are the air I breathe

because when I don't see you for a long time

my chest tightens

you complete me

when I am with you

I feel like I can do anything

and take on anyone

you make me feel like

I am the most beautiful woman God created

you give me strength I never knew I had

and for that

I love you!

S.L.Branch

3/24/02

*S. LaTisha Branch*

# How Much Love

She come home after work
and tries to fix a decent meal
She cooks and cleans
and still makes love like a queen
Constantly making sure you are ok
never complains, argues or fights.
She loves you whether you are wrong or right
She supports you in what you want to do
and she stands by you if it happens to fall through
She loves you much more than you love her
because she loves with all of herself
and she loves you for being you
She tries to make you happy
in everything she does
so love her
appreciate her
and never let her go

    S.L.Branch

    3/29/02

# My Knight

I watch you sit at the table
looking at me with sad brown eyes
just wishing that I could
take it all away
looking as good as a "GQ" centerfold
in a black turtleneck that
hugs your cuddly, yet masculine body
and neatly tucks into you well fitted pants
as I hold your hand to touch my face
I feel all the task those hands do
from home, work and play
then I lay my head on your shoulder
and let out a sigh or relief
because I know that I am at the safest place
now all that is left is for you to
put your arms around me
and then I know that no one can reach me
and nothing can hurt me
until that day when you walk away
and never come back
I will wait for the day when I never see you walk away.

# No Love Loss

Why do I still love you?

You kept me happy when it counted

I had an ongoing smile that was true

love, affection and time was on my side

you made me feel like I was a queen and untouchable

then you touched me and I broke

you broke me into unfixable pieces

you hurt me, and let me down

so why do I still love the man that hurt me so bad

because when you loved me you loved me so good

so yes, I still love you. I just don't respect you.

S.L.Branch

10/15/00

# Life's Stairway

As I climb the stairs of life I see
A lot of obstacles surrounding me
lift the foot for the first step
and say to everyone "I Don't need no help"
tough and as unsteady as it seems
I keep trying to fulfill all my dreams
the more steps I take and make
I feel my spirit they want to break
each day getting harder to cope
there has got to be a better day, I hope
all I want is to be happy
and love someone that love me

S.L.Branch

8/15/00

# Policewoman

All dressed in navy blue, ready for the street
with silver on her chest, and a gun on her hip to beat
innocence in the face, but attitude for days
her job she will do and using her own ways
there may be struggle and hard times to come
but she will show them where she's from.

S.L.Branch

4/00

# My Day

Sitting in that room starring at the wall

is this really me or just a bad call

waiting to be made into the princess that is in me

girls all around, making my face, curling my hair

as the butterflies flutter in my stomach, my head's in a whirl

is this day finally here, or is this just a dream

fixing the girdle, putting on the hose, and adjusting the rest

making sure you look your best, in each and every way

why? Because this is supposed to be your special day

putting on the finishing touches and adding the last little flair

as the girls put that glittering, shimmering tiara in your hair

now your ready girl to go and show the world

The prize for the luckiest man in the world.

S.L.Branch

2/23/00

# Yes, But No

What do we have in this relationship we are in?
The nights we spend together I feel I'm livin in sin.
I care for you with all my heart,
but a real relationship we just can't start.
I want more than just your satisfied,
with the fact of just being occupied.
An occasional dinner or night on the town,
keeps my smile from being a frown.
And a night of sexual bliss,
keeps you on my emotion list.

S.L. Branch

2/23/00

# The Way I Feel

I can't do anything but love you
I have nothing else to give
I would love to give you the world
when all I have to give is me

I love you so much words can't say
how my heart and soul feels
the way your smile brightens up my day
and your voice lightens my way

I don't know why I am so afraid
to let myself go
I trust you more than you know
I never want to see you go

When we part I want to take a piece of you
So I know that no matter what we are together
I somehow feel empty without you
like a shell with no muscle
S.L.Branch
01/21/00

# You Belong To Her

When you'll call me back later,
or when you just have to make a run.
You belong to her...

When you don't call right back,
or just go into the other room.
You belong to her...

I know were I stand when you say,
"I'm just talking to one of the guys".
You belong to her...

When you are questioned and answer,
each and every questions.
You belong to her...

When the people walk and look,
and we move or stop conversation.
You belong to her...

When you can't be away from home,
and not answer a page or call without catching grief.
You belong to her...

When your car can't be at another house
or another car can't be at your house.
You belong to her...

How do I know? Because what she wants she gets,
as the great Malcolm X said, "By any means necessary".
And until you stop the vicious circle, you will belong to her.
S.L.Branch
01/5/00

# What am I

I love her

She was the best and the worst thing that ever happen to me

First my parents gave her to me

While growing up she was given to me all the time

So much so that I had to give her away, As much as possible

But I needed her just as much as I gave her away

The older I got I needed her in different ways more and more

When I started dating she was given and taken away

Taken more than given

The more dating I did the worst my needs would get

She's wanted, needed and required

She is what every girls dreams of and every boy needs

She is what everyone should have and what only some truly get.

I want her to love me

S. L. Branch

5/20/03

# How I Died

The day you first took my hand

and said I am your friend

I wanted no part of you

or your heart

your help and concern

made my nerves burn

The more I pushed away

the more you pushed to stay

You stood by me without even knowing

and my inner self started showing

How could he care and not really know me

How could he support me and not the father be

You stayed by my side as if I was carrying your child

My situation was all but mild.

As days passed my feelings grew

But I never knew what you would put me through

When the bad news came

you loved me just the same

I let myself go and loved you back

although the odds against us were stacked

you said you wanted forever

and me by your side in all kinds of weather

Then came the bomb, that hit me

like a bullet through my heart

I begged you not to hurt me

and that promise you made to thee

When you broke that promise

you may as well have shot me dead

because again I believed every lie you said

So I hope you had fun killing me again inside

because for the last time, I DIED.

S.L.Branch

2003

# Dedication

I would first like to give honor and thanks to "God" for giving me the strength and endurance to allow me to accomplish my goals and keep going over mountains and through valleys.

I would like to dedicate this book in memory of the late Herbert Lee and Alma O'Neal White, my grandparents who instilled in our family greatness. Also, the late Vanessa Faye Ruff, my aunt who supported every crazy idea and professed that I could do no wrong. Lastly, the late Timothy Joel Branch, my father who along with my mother loved and raised me to be the woman that I am today. This book is in their memory, thanking them for years of support and guidance through good and trying times.

To my children, Daisha, Demetrius and Deondre' (Triple Threat), I thank you for teaching me patience, and unconditional love. I am raising you the best that I know how and praying along the way. Just know that I love you no matter what, and you can do and be anything you set your little hearts on. You have given my life a whole new meaning. I LOVE YOU MORE!

To my mother, Consuelo Jan White Branch, I would like to thank you for all your support, guidance, encouragement, love and mostly for raising me to be the strong independent woman that I am. Thank you for keeping me spiritually grounded. You led me to God and he guided me. I know I have not done all that you expected of me, but I am your child. You are my mother, my nurse, my protector, and my heart. I LOVE YOU MORE, MORE, MORE!

To my soul mate/friend, I must thank you for standing by me and supporting me when the others would not and loving me the best that you know how. Also for being a male role model in their life for all you do, I love you.

To my special cousin Calvina D. Ruff, Uncle Calvin, Aunt Althea and the rest of my family in Virginia, North Carolina and all over, I love you all, FAMILY FIRST.

I would also like to thank those who have been fortunate to be called my friends. In some way or another you have helped strengthen me. To the men who have been fortunate enough to be apart of my life, I hope that these words give you insight on appreciating the finer things in life. When you obtain that one person treat her as though she is that diamond that is worth all the money in the world. To the men that will meet me in the future, take note and come correct. If you remember to always respect me and you will always be respected. Finally, to all those women who have loved and lost and think this is it. Well, IT'S NOT!

Much Love,
S. LaTisha Branch

# About The Author

Suenyo LaTisha Branch, is a 30-year-old mother to three children known to most as simply "Tisha". She is a down to earth, quiet yet opinionated person. She has five Godchildren, three nieces, and two nephews. She is the oldest daughter to Consuelo J.W. the late Timothy Joel Branch. Tisha's life is full of activity with a two-year-old active little girl and two boys, ages 6 and 8 that are all boy. A very young, loving and supportive mother who is a three-year breast cancer survivor and at 53 is helping Tisha raise these three children, along with taking care of Tisha's aunt, whom is slightly delayed. So her home and life are very full right now.

Printed in the United States
By Bookmasters